A Song For You...
The Darker Side Of Life

Lyn Hansen-Blizzárd

Order this book online at www.trafford.com
or email orders@trafford.com

Most Trafford titles are also available at major online book retailers.

Note for Librarians: A cataloguing record for this book is available from Library
and Archives Canada at www.collectionscanada.ca/amicus/index-e.html

Printed in the United States of America.

ISBN: 978-1-4269-7598-1 (sc)
ISBN: 978-1-4269-7599-8 (e)

Trafford rev. 08/10/2011

 www.trafford.com

North America & international
toll-free: 1 888 232 4444 (USA & Canada)
phone: 250 383 6864 ♦ fax: 812 355 4082

I want to thank those who said to me, "write what you know" or "just write, it will come" ... it did. Thanks to those who took time out of their busy schedules to read, comment and then nudge me to get this published.

To those who have lived the words within these pages and allowed me to share in their darker side of life – thank you!

A very special thank you to my "sister friend" who always reminded me that dreams can come true even when I had all but given up hope that this book would become a reality.

Thank you reader for joining me in taking a look at the darker side of life, never forgetting that in the end, there will always be a song.

This book is dedicated to anyone and everyone who has experienced the darker side of life. Darkness comes in many guises. It may be an addiction, mental or emotional illness, suicide, old age, terminal illness, abuse, death, or just plain loneliness. Chances are that none of us escapes this life without coming face to face with the darker side of life. It may come to a friend, a loved one, or to you yourself. The good news is that there is always a song to be sung, even in the darkest night.

Preface

The ability to feel what another feels transcends age, sex, race, or cultural boundaries. To think and feel another persons pain is both a blessing and a curse at times. I have been told countless times that I have this ability. I believe it stems from a prayer I prayed many years ago as a teenager. I asked God to break my heart with things that broke His heart... these poems are a result of that breaking heart.

"Lyn gives a voice to those feelings that are not easily expressed... allowing us all to share the human experience."

Deborah and Nick Tyzio. The Land of Deborah, Musician And Sound Engineer

A Song For You...

I sing a song for you
Of the darker side of life
Days of heartache, pain and sorrow
Of loneliness and strife

I sing a song for you
Of a body broken down
A ravaged mind, confused, alone
A voice uttering not a sound

I sing a song for you
Of sleepless nights of fear
Hours filled with anguish
A life void of hope or cheer

I sing a song for you
Of a brighter happy day
When your angst is finally over
And your peace has come to stay

What is the darker side of life
Is it when a man beats his wife
When a teenager overdoses on drugs
And there's no one who cares that he does
Could the darker side of life perhaps be
A body racked in pain for all to see
A once bright mind now at a loss
When a child is beaten to prove who's boss
A life devoid of anything fun
So the life is ended by the click of a gun
Hopelessness, loneliness, a life of despair
Wondering if there's anyone, anywhere who cares
Who can they turn to, where can they go
Surely there must be someone who knows
Searching for answers, searching for love
Longing to connect with God above

"You feel the pain of the whole world is coming through these words."

Rupert Macnee, Media/Market Consultant

A Song For The Fading Mind...

"Sometimes in the day to day grind of caregiving, I lose that part of me that feels. These pages bring me back."

Steve Austin, Spouse and Caregiver

Memories fade as memories do
But tell me why I can't remember you
You seem to know me or at least who I was
Fleeting faces all turn into a fuzz
Trapped in a world I know nothing of
Yet deep, deep inside me I remember love

Try as hard as I can I don't remember your name
Do we look alike are we one in the same
What is happening to me kind stranger do tell
I feel that I'm falling down a deep dark well
Trapped in a world I know nothing of
Yet deep, deep inside me I remember love

You hold my arm and you guide my hand
My thoughts are scattered searching for a place to land
Wait just a moment a glimmer of light
We've loved one another, isn't that right
Trapped in a world I know nothing of
Yet deep, deep inside me I remember love

Maybe just maybe I'm not totally lost
Can you help me kind stranger am I worth the cost
Trapped in a world I know nothing of
Yet deep, deep inside me I remember love
Trapped in a world I know nothing of
Yet deep, deep inside me I remember your love

Where, oh where have you gone
My partner, my darling, my wife
A mere shadow of who you once were
My friend and the love of my life

Together we've flown to foreign cities
And we've sailed to distant shores
We've had many good times together
Yet now we'll fly and sail no more

We struggle each day just to live
Every morning new challenges we face
I'm weary sometimes and just want to quit
But I remember your love and pray for more grace

Everyday brings new heartaches
With memories of what use to be
And I know it won't be much longer
'Til you won't even remember me

Where, oh where have you gone
My partner, my darling, my wife
A mere shadow of who you once were
I miss you, love of my life

Reader's Notes

A Song For The Lost...

Half eaten food on an abandoned tray
Is a banquet to a guy from the streets
A moth eaten blanket from a garbage dump
For the homeless is like satin sheets

Don't be too quick to judge them
Not all are junkies you know
Some were people just like you
Who never thought they'd sink so low

The stroke of a pen and a job is gone
An investment goes down the drain
The bank calls the loan and your house is gone
You find yourself out in the rain

So next time you pass that homeless guy
Or the woman begging for a little change
Realize that but for the grace of God
You and they could be one in the same

The old house now stands empty
A shell of what once held dear
Flowers still gown beside it
But no one's lived there in years

The old house holds many a story
Of youth, young love and joys
Candles once fit every window
The yard was filled with toys

The old house stands abandoned
It stares blankly at the sea
In some strange way it's a reminder
The old house is a shadow of me

The streets where the lonely walk
Are alive with sounds of the night
Lost souls hovering in the shadows
Afraid to face the morning light

An old woman pushes a grocery cart
Holding everything she holds dear
Clutching tightly the collar of a worn out coat
Living out her days in fear

An old man staggers down an alley way
Can't remember when last he ate
Staring at the Mission up ahead
Wondering when they'll open the gate

Refuge awaits just beyond the doors
Warmth and safety lie ahead
Is there room enough for all
Or in the morning will some be dead

The streets where the lonely walk
Are alive with sounds of the night
Lost souls hovering in the shadows
Afraid to face the morning light

Reader's Notes

"Lyn's poems speak to the stark pain of life boldly and plainly. Her phrases evoke a bittersweet sadness in one breath and then save you from the very same in the next by filling it with hope."

Catherine Lough Hagguist, Actress and Owner of Biz Books

A Song For The Troubled Spirit...

Faces swirling all around me laughing
Mocking saying naught
Hands unseen pushing pulling dreadful
Feelings of being caught

Overwhelming helpless bondage
Tearing at my very core
Without help and blessed freedom
I shall simply exist no more

Sacred hallways leading nowhere
Every turn the same
Empty caverns total darkness
Have I finally gone insane

Questions burning ever burning
Yet no one seems to tell
I'm falling ever downward
I'm on a journey straight to hell

Why did you do it
I need to know
Was life that bad
Was it filled with woe

How blind we all were
To your deep inner pain
How your world was crumbling
How you felt insane

If you only had told us
A little at least
Then maybe together
We could have crushed the beast

Gone are the chances now
To ever help
Now I live in guilt
Trying to grasp the pain you felt

Why did you do it
I need to know
Was life so bad
Was it filled with woe

A troubled soul
Just playing a role
Void of any family or friend

A face in a glass
Just one of the mass
Searching for a way to mend

This too shall pass
For nothing lasts
Everything must come to an end

A troubled soul
Just playing a role
Yet a new life waits 'round the bend

Acid and speed are bad they say
Claim the price will be hard to pay
Burns our minds out for all time
But look at me, I'm doin' fine

Tried everything on the streets and in school
Nothing but the best, buddy, I'm no fool
I may enjoy it but I'm no junkies' clown
I could stop if I wanted, I just fool around

Try it all at least once, my friend once said
Funny but that friend of mine now is dead
Maybe there's something to stoppin' afterall
Guess I'm getting' tired of dodgin' the law

Wonder who would help me if I really tried
Tried to talk to Mom once, she just cried
Guess she thinks she failed me and Dad does too
Doesn't really matter now, I'm lost and that's true

Screamin' out for mercy to a God they say does care
I can't see or hear Him, is He really there?
Can He really help me, is there a hope –
Or will I die a loser, hooked on Dope?

One joint too many, one beer too much
The head goes funny, way out of touch
Round and round the pistol goes
Who's gonna die nobody knows
Kids playing games they know nothing of
They wanna be cool, they just seek love

An empty bottle on the table
A glass half full on a shelf
Wanting to quit but not yet able
Too afraid to even face myself

I turn to a Higher Power
Facing emotions I have felt
Now is the deciding hour
As all my excuses melt

While I listen to other stories
I hear my own every day
I lay no claim to fame or glory
But I feel that I'm on my way

Reader's Notes

A Song For The Children...

Little girl lost where have you gone
Where is the light in your eyes
Sitting alone no one in sight
Just you and the fireflies

Little boy lost where have you gone
You stare blankly in a daze
Sitting alone no one in sight
The world around you all ablaze

I hear the footsteps and I cringe
I know they've been on an all night binge
Very soon I'll feel nothing but pain
My pleading cries are all in vain
Will my daily terror ever end
When will God my guardian angel send
One more blow and I'll forever sleep
Over my lifeless form they'll stand and weep
They'll finally stagger out into the yard
Wondering why they had to hit so very hard
Someone will bury me neath soft green sod
And I will sleep forever in the arms of God

Reader's Notes

"These words are like dancing to the edge of one's senses, and deep into one's, everyone's, bank of memory."

Rupert Macnee, Media/Market Consultant

A Song For The Broken Family...

Angry voices grow much louder
No one hears the small child cry
Clutching tightly a worn out teddy
Not really understanding why
Mommy yells at Daddy
Daddy yells at Mommy too
Grown up words the child can't fathom
What can a small child do
Daddy grabs his keys and turns to leave
Now he's heading out the door
With teary eyes Mommy hugs her
And whispers, "Daddy doesn't live here anymore"

I turn around and you are gone
I ask myself what went wrong
I try to find courage to go on
To live again to have a song
To embrace the day to face the dawn
To find a place where I belong

Clutching her rag doll
A little girl cries
Her Daddy is leaving
She can't understand why
He smiles at her sweetly
But there's tears in his eyes
Don't forget Daddy loves you
Is all he can say
He picks up his bags
And he's gone away
She stares out the window
This is a horrible day

Holding his puppy
A little boy stares
Mommy is crying
Daddy just glares
Out in the street
A car horn blares
Be strong little man
Mommy says with a kiss
Always remember I love you
And it's you I will miss
Just leave if you're going
Daddy shouts with a hiss

It's the children who suffer
When a marriage goes wrong
The adults bounce back
They just sing a different song
It's the littlest victim
Who wonder what they did wrong
It's not their fault
But they don't understand
She was his little princess
He was her little man
Now the world around them
Becomes sinking sand

"Dear Lyn, Inside suffering, there is a secret. It is discovered in the silence of the open, surrendered heart. And as your beautiful poems show, the secret... is love."

Peter Kyne, MD

A Song For The Aged...

Time has past, the day is done
Gone is the daylight, gone is the sun
Another day over, another day spent
Can't help but wonder, where all the time went

An old man sits in his rocking chair
Wondering where time has gone
Running his finger through his thinning hair
Remembering briefly an old love song

An old woman struggles to get out of bed
Another lonely day to start
Arthritic hands rub a tired forehead
Remembering briefly the love of her heart

An old man and an old woman
Walk ever so slowly hand in hand
In silence they go not wanting or able to talk
Afar, in the distance they softly hear a band

Melodious music like they've never heard
Sweeter music than the songs of a bird
Welcoming them to a home far away
A place of comfort where they forever will stay

A Song For The Dying...

My body may be broken
Yet my spirit soars on high
My song is but a token
Of my future by and by

Soon my suffering will be over
And I'll rest on golden shores
Beside fields of flowers and clover
My pain will be no more

I'll close my eyes and go to sleep
To wake in heaven above
Those left behind I'm sure will weep
When I join the One I love

We'll sing and dance on streets of gold
With and angels I will sing
My sweet Lord I shall behold
And I'll worship Him as my King

I come to you on silver wings
That glimmer in the sun
And as I fly through cloudless skies
I know that we are one
Gone are the things I once have known
They fade more every day
Yet as I go I'm not afraid
I know it's all okay
My new life stands before me
My battles here are done
I know you wait to greet me
For we are truly one

"These words, very visual, very emotive are meant to be heard and also to be seen."

Rupert Macnee, Media/Market Consultant

Keeping with the nomad life style of her Viking and Native ancestry, Lyn Hansen Blizzárd has lived in Europe, Canada and several US States. She currently resides in Blaine, WA.

Lyn is the author of one other book, "My A-Z Color Me Book" and has been published in various periodicals.

Readers Notes